Blurred Vision

Original Poetry

Written by

Carlos Harleaux

Find additional poetry at www.peauxeticexpressions.com
Contact: Peauxetic.Expressions@gmail.com

Dedication and Acknowledgments

I would like to dedicate this book to everyone who has inspired me to write its contents. Whether it was good or bad inspiration, it was needed to help me complete the work in front of you today, and I'm thankful.

I also want to thank my parents (Debra and Ronnie Swisher and Carl Harleaux), my grandparents (Jean and Collins Kyle), as well as the rest of my family, all of who have loved me, supported me and believed in me; they have all helped to steer me to this appointed place in time! And to my special lady, Alexandria Hatcher, for her never ending support!

I want to thank my close friends John Adams, Bruce August, Jr., Desmond Blair, Michelle Buggs, Arthur Gregg, Tammie Henry, Joshua Story, and Andre Wallace. These friends, among many others, have really pushed me to pursue the completion of this book and I thank them for it.

Last, but certainly not least, I thank God, for His love, guidance and direction! Thanks to those who have had a major influence on my spiritual life; Pastors T. Murray, S. Duckens and J. McNeil.

Although I wasn't able to specifically name everyone one, I thank each of you reading this book for your support. If I forgot anyone, please blame it on my head and not my heart.

Blurred Vision
Table of Contents

Gray Matter
Guess Who, Guess What
Dirty Laundry
Fools (Me or You)

Blurred Vision
All That Glitters
Erase
Game Over
Buzz
Another Love
Because of You

Don't Know
The Gates of Destiny
Missionary Love
Stronghold
The Weakest Link
Until The Next Time
Tired
Clocking Out
The Taste of Love
Sound of Silence

The Sleep In Generation
Angels Unaware
Broken
Through My Eyes

Introduction

The human eye takes in an enormous amount of visuals every day. Our brain continually processes these images and some of them are even subconscious snapshots we don't know that we've seen. Just think about how many words, pictures, commercials, and gestures we take in daily. Even today's marketing capitalizes on our desire for viewing pleasure with 3D images and high tech graphics. Our eyes are so important and help us make informed decisions and decipher what is pleasing to us.

For some of us, we may need a little help reaching the 20/20 vision we are supposed to have. I have what is called nearsighted vision, which allows you to see objects up close, but not at a distance. This condition is actually how I came up with the title and concept of my book. How many times have we been in situations where we evaluate our projected success based on what's right in front of us? As I have learned and continue to learn, this could not be a more uninformed assumption. I have had to bump my head in the past to realize the bigger picture is usually the better picture. But I'm thankful for it, because it helped me write the book in front of you today.

Without my contacts or glasses, I feel blind. My vision is just a blur and I only take out my contacts or remove my glasses right before I go to sleep. There are times in life, many of which are detailed in the poems here, where I "didn't have my glasses on." I started realizing a pattern of developing various unhealthy situations, and feeling helpless to those around me that may have been experiencing the same thing. I was blinded by a warped perception and because my vision was blurred, I didn't see a clear way out.

Every poem in this book is personal and is either something I have felt at one point or learned from watching those close to me. Through my mistakes and setbacks, I was able to find release in writing. Now, here I am today, more wise than before but still under construction. Aren't we all though? My desire is that you are moved, motivated, convicted and inspired by the contents of *Blurred Vision*. Even better, maybe it will help you correct the vision in your life to prepare you for your best potential.

Behind A Smile

What mysteries rest behind a smile?

And what stories lie unrevealed behind a laugh?

Those who appear to be happy

Aren't always as they seem

Sometimes I feel as though

I am the one hiding behind myself

Sometimes I don't feel like talking

I don't feel like laughing

But you gotta smile through it

Because that's what people expect

Your smile is therapy to others

But where's the relaxation for you?

Who knows what goes on?

Who knows what battles have to be won?

Who knows what problems are masked?

Who knows who is really happy?

Or just hiding behind a smile?

Content

Content, that's what we are
Little do we know
We create our own invisible scars
That's why we as a people
Will never rise
Until we remove
Until we remove
Until we remove
The veil of excuses
From our eyes
We settle for less
Not knowing we're the best
Lazy mentalities have put
So many of us to rest
We complain
We cry
We criticize
And we whine
All the while
Sitting on our butts
Eroding away the time
Time that could be used successfully
Is instead thrown away so destructively
And at the end of the day
We must realize
We create our own catastrophes

2 The Hard Way

When I treat you good
You run away
I turn around and then
You beg to stay
When I'm there for you
You disconnect the line
But when I ignore you
You act better every time
You would think these things
Wouldn't happen the way they do
But the more I think about
I realize I'll never understand you
1 is the loneliest number
And 3 is too much company
But 2, with me and you
Is beginning to take
Too much out of me

Caution

Running fast in pursuit of an empty space
No substance will be gained in getting to this destination
Still I refuse to pump the brakes
And detour to a more familiar place
Where I should be
Instead of this trap that feels like quicksand
And I suggest, that unless you want to sink in too
You let go of my hand
Disobeying the traffic signals
Just so I can break through the inner city limits
To this wonderful place of nowhere special
To this place of cruel intentions
Approaching the bridge of murky water
And eerie silence
Somehow my excitement is not the same
Yet I am not ashamed
So I keep on moving
Finally crossing the bridge as the gate greets me
Only to realize I don't need an overnight stay
To realize this ain't the place to be

So Sick

The highest pinnacle

Doesn't compare to these trenches

I am not myself and this feeling

Of healing and injury is unproductive

This piece of a promise is beneath me

And I am better than this

Better than reducing my being

By seeming so vulnerable

Intolerable, I tell myself

Is what I will be of this labyrinth

Yet here I am again

Searching, Wishing, Hoping, Dreaming

Desperate…can't you feel my heart beaming?

With pride and joy laced with pleasure and pain

That provides a dry haven for confusion to reign

But I am ready to gain so I will

Lose this baggage

That has crippled my destiny

Shackled my victories

Kept me bound to insecurities

Because to keep doing the same thing

Over and over again with you

Is truly the definition of insanity

Invisible Chains

I am bound to the floor
Looking through a glass ceiling
That crumbles at the touch
If only I could reach it…
In some instances
The only one keeping me bound is me
Not bound by tangible shackles, chains or walls
But limited to undetectable dimensions
Where I can barely stand
I will not break free before my time
So I get comfortable
In the uncomfortable feeling of being bound
Hearing the sound of clanking metal with each movement
This becomes my soundtrack,
Drowned out by other
Distractions that keep me busy
The noise is sometimes better
Than the reality of the silence
But for today, I will embrace this tangled web…
Accept the strain, and know
It's all personal gain in the end
To ascend I know I must
Endure the growing pains of
Breaking loose from these
Invisible chains

1 Life 2 Live

You only have one life to live
So how will you live it?
Do you make the most of the hand
You've been dealt?
Or do you wallow in the
Waters of pity?
Don't give up on the life
God breathed into you
Troubles may come
But in the morning
Happiness will be plentiful
It's just so unbeautiful
To see someone take their life
Over just a few burdens
Their soul brutally murdered
But don't give up on life
Don't give up on you
When you die it should be natural
Not by trigger pulling, taking pills,
Or wrist slitting
Open the windows of your soul
Air out your frustrations
Before they turn cold
Don't waste the precious time you have now
Stressing about the past
Hold on to the present and
Try to make that last
Change what you can
Accept what you can't
You can make it if you try
Choose to live
It's not up to you to
Make the choice to die

"Sometimes you have to reflect on your past to prepare for your future. Hindsight is 20/20."

Carlos Harleaux

Photos of the Soul

She used to be the epitome of love

Now her jagged portrait hangs on the wall

But it wasn't always jagged and was

Even once polished and shiny

But not anymore

The film started to get grungy

The dirt caked on is hard to remove

I tried Tide, Bleach and Comet

But my heart is still left un-soothed

If only you could behold her beauty

In the un-blurred sense

Before it turned into this

If only I could take the picture once more

Then maybe you would see

But I guess I'm out on my luck

Because I ran out of film

She fell from the panoramic view of my soul

Without even leaving me the proofs

Maybe she did not want me to make duplicates

Because that would have been too much information

I just wish you could see her before she developed into this

Her photo is now beyond recognition, but I keep it anyway

Because it's all I have left to reminisce

Nobody But Somebody

I wanna send you an invitation
To my emancipation
I wanna thank you for being you
That allowed me to see a better me
I wanna let you know
You didn't bring me down
But the lack of love you showed
Only saved room for more of me to go around
I've healed your wounds with
The remedy of real happiness
But I wanna thank you for showing me
How it should be done

You showed me how to love someone
How to kiss someone
How to touch someone
Be missed by someone
You showed me what it feels
To have somebody to love
You showed me that nobody
But somebody deserves to be my number one

I wanna purchase your front row seat
To my headlining show
I wanna apologize for wasting time
That we both knew was well spent
I wanna give her all the things
You never gave to me
I wanna make her happy like
Better than the way we used to be
Now you've shown me just the way love goes
And finally, I'm in control

You showed me how to love someone
How to hug someone
How to make love and someone
Deserves all I have to offer
How to forgive someone
To have somebody who cares
You showed me you deserve nobody
But a special somebody to be your number one

Letters of the Ghostlover

The depth of our relationship
Has mainly been in writing
I'm tired of these communicative roadblocks
So I'm throwing away my pen
Conveying my heartfelt message
You told me you loved me
But only in letters
If I could hear you speak the words
I would feel so much better
Hiding behind lines, spaces and margins
When I lend a listening ear
This is how you dodge it
Packing away your timid heart
Hiding it in the closet
Well, I'm ending writing letters
I want more than emotions on paper
I want to see it
I want to hear it
I want to feel it
But since I can't, this will be my last letter
I keep this my own secret
Just too bad you'll never get to read it

Red Light

You've been calling me
Everyday and all hours of the night
Then showing up at my spot
Unannounced, knowing that ain't right
Checking where I am
Asking questions, saying who is this?
When you already know
That we're not in a relationship
Now if I acted a fool
Turned my back and called you out your name
There'd be no ifs, ands or buts about this
I'd be the one to blame
Tried to let you know
Break it down and be polite
But now I see that I'm gon'
Have to give you the Red Light

Whoa, pump your brakes
It's not that serious
You gotta slow down
Because you're making me delirious
Whoa, get your feet off the gas
Get your feet of the gas
Moving way too fast
Get your feet off the gas

Now you already know my personality
Is chilled as ice
But if you think you got me
You better think twice
Because I'm not for commitment
Locking down and throw away the key
So all your little games ain't
Even helping to persuade me
Don't you have to work?
Wash some clothes?

Or go clean up your house?
Well, why are you here?
No disrespect but can you exit now?
You're running stop signs
No yielding to the yellow lights
Gotta turn them hazards on
And turn off the brights

Whoa, pump your brakes
It's not that serious
You gotta slow down
Because you're making me delirious
Whoa, get your feet off the gas
Get your feet of the gas

Oh, can't you see
You're really buggin me
Gotta let you know
Before you make me go crazy
It's past due for us
To sit and discuss
That I ain't in love
Because it was all about lust

Throwback

Like your favorite rocking chair
Like that old T-shirt I wear
So comfortable, so familiar
Like reservations for two
I still remember how it was with you
So free, and so special
It's like "That's your side of the bed"
It's like all the funny things you said
Like the way you used to look at me
Like how it was and felt for us to be in

Throwback love
That one and only true (love)
The one you'll always cut for
You're head over heels for
Whenever you need
You know I'm here
Throwback girl
You are my world
Ain't nothing like that throwback love

Like leftovers on my plate
Like those old school jams we used to play
No worries, no complications
Like all the times you said it was over
I'm drunk off of you
And I don't wanna be sober
No insecurities, no arguments
It's like that spark that's in your kiss
It's like your picture as I reminisce
Like how we used to break it down
Like how I can't deny
I miss having you around for

Throwback love
That one and only true (love)
The one you'll always cut for
You're head over heels for
Whenever you need
You know I'm here
Throwback girl
You are my world
Ain't nothing like that throwback love

Throwback love
(Could we get it back?)
Is what I really miss
(Is it too late?)
Throwback love
(Wondering if you)
Is what I gotta have
(Feel the same way too)

Drunk Off Your Love

There you go

Sitting there looking sweet and cool

Thought I had it under control

But I can't get enough of you

It goes down nice and easy

And then it makes me trip and stumble

I should have known your love was no good

Right from the very start

Intoxicated and liberated

In this euphoric state

You got my heart burning

And reality keeps checking in late

Delusional, confusional

Feeling so disoriented

I think I need a break from you

To recoup some of my sanity

I need a glass of water to

Wash away the pain

But there I go again taking another sip

Clearly I'm outta control and

I need to get away from you.

Puppet

Every time I think I've gotten away

These strings keep pulling me back to the stage

Where I put on this show you control

Every night I pray for the final encore

But this invisible crowd seems to roar and yell for more

I'm tired of this performance

So I'll wait until the intermission to escape

I need a get away

Even if it's only a temporary one

If I could cut these strings

I would have more control

If I could cut these strings

I wouldn't feel so low

Restless is my adjective of choice

For another night brings another show

Another show brings another devastating

Blow of reality

That I could have been released from this captivity

A long time ago....if I had just asked to be free

I had never looked up to see

That the puppet in control of my agony was

Me

Slave

I've been working these fields
All night and all day
But when the sun goes down
No one sees the change
Hating on me because I'm
The designated "house nigga"
Or so you think
Well, just to let you know
This plantation does not define me
Because I knew my worth
Before my first seed was sown
Before my cells became full grown
Alone
I may not have gash marks or open
Wounds lined across my back
My feet may not be calloused
And my face may not be slashed
But when master comes to see us
Are we not all slaves?
Just because what happened to you
Over yonder did not happen
On my side of town
That gives you no right to treat me
Like less of a man and constantly put me down
Negative reinforcement is what some call it
But to me it's just an excuse to buy time
Stalling and ignoring the simple fact that is
Traced back into generations past
We're still those same slave NIGGERS who they
Packed like sardines in trucks
Then tied us up together and made us
Stand in line
Let it not surprise you
That knowledge can be gained
Without torture and pain
I still know the storm is coming

Though I may not have felt the rain
Did you not notice the way I walk with pride?
Whether bloody, bruised or tattered
My head will always remain high
Trace back through the history to see
That's what we were really meant to be
Servants, caring and receptive to the needs of others
Not exploiting
Not despising
Not judging
Not fighting within ourselves
Amongst ourselves
And easily divided
Don't you get it?
Don't you see?
Slave Mentality

Respect

What is respect?
And what does it mean to you?
Do you let the opinion of others
Dictate everything you do?
If I choose to ignore you
Calling me out my name
Does that mean that you neglect to
Respect the fact that I am a person
Or would I be disrespecting myself
If I rebutted just the same
Respect is the key that unlocks
Caged souls
Winning trust is not easy
And sometimes to get respect
You have to step outside your comfort zone
Cool, calm, militant, angry, just
Step back
Our own kind does not
Want to remain eye level
So when they walk past you
They pull down their hats
Respect? Yourself?
You gotta learn to love you
Cause at the end of the day
It means nothing if the stress of trying to
Gain respect has made a respectable fool outta you
But it's cool to play the fool
When everybody's feeling you, right?

Wrong! turns of self worth
Have murdered many and left
Infinite souls burnt
To a crisp as I sit and
Observe all that surrounds me
I wonder will I float on the crest of
Limitless standards, uncompromising
Even if standing alone?
Or will I let respect neglect the
Fact that I am somebody
And swallow me whole?

Hold Me Down

I can't win in this battle
I won't keep up the fight
About to go insane
And it's all because of you
Every time I need you to be
A little more supportive of me
You're not around
Nowhere to be found
Drowned in your own problems
While I'm expected to brush it off
Like it's okay

I don't mind holding you up
Whenever you're in need
But every day's a new dilemma
That's detrimental to me
You only care about yourself
And something's got to give
I bring you up, you hold me down
That's not the way to live

No matter what the scenario
It's always worse than mine
If you could step outside of selfishness
Maybe you could actually see
That every time I need you to be
A little more supportive of me
Your head's hanging down
Your soul's under the ground
And I ask myself when is this gonna end?
Cause I can't keep up the fight

I don't mind holding you up
Whenever you're in need
But every day's a new dilemma
That's detrimental to me

You only care about yourself
And something's got to give
I bring you up, you hold me down
That's not the way to live

Should've known from the beginning
Guess I ignored the signs
I should have paid more attention
But I just have a few questions
So who's gonna be around
For you to cry on their shoulder?
Who's gonna give you comfort
Self sacrificing
When your heart feels cold?
Nobody

I don't mind holding you up
Whenever you're in need
But every day's a new dilemma
That's detrimental to me
You only care about yourself
And something's got to give
I bring you up, you hold me down
That's not the way to live

This task is draining
With no reciprocity
Your love's taking me over
And it's about to get the best of me

"You'll never get to where you need to be, if you can't envision yourself being there."

Carlos Harleaux

News Flash

Her blood stains the door
She lazily slides to the floor
The pain in her chest told her
She couldn't deal with this anymore
Now we're reporting live
With cameras on the scene
Another day, another statistic
If you know what I mean
She told him to stop
As he beat her to the ground
She'd be able to sleep at night
If it wasn't for that sound
No witnesses questioned
But no silence heard
They did that all the time
Or at least that was the word
Fragments of brain splattered
Scattered on the window pane
And after that night they both
Would never be the same
The top story at 10:00
Seems domestic violence is in
But he shouldn't have turned his back this time
Because this is the one fight he wouldn't win

Conversation With God

Some scholars may say
Einstein had it all figured out
Erykah Badu and her ankh…
Whatever that is
Got the New Amerykah…she and Obama
Just in case you were in doubt
Freud had the key to unlock the mind
But who do I call on
When the rent's past due?
And the light bill's behind?
He has power over all
And If I had the chance I'd want to have
A conversation with God
Not converse with Him over
An herb crusted salmon
But keep it real like
Greens and cornbread
Like the rib of me
Ask Him who will be my Eve?
And even though I'm not worthy
What does He think of me?
Could He give me a progress report?
And let me know what I need to improve on
To make it in?
I'd thank Him for His mercy
From troubles seen and unseen
For all the things that happened for a
Reason that I may never know
Ask Him how many times
Does He flee from me
When my temple doesn't provide a home?
Is this the Revelation
We're living in today?
Ask Him why our loved ones had to go
So soon?

Different

You must feel so secure

And content with your normality

To put us down like

You are so perfect, in all totality

We know the difference

And we feel the pain

We are the all stars of this league

But you invented the game

How would you feel if

By our lips, your names were burned?

Spend a day in our shoes

Then maybe you'll learn

Try a lifetime as an outcast

Then maybe you could understand that we

Are different from you

But yet and still the same

We shine through the struggles

To become the ones who blow out your

Dimly lit flame

Didn't Ask For This

I didn't ask to be your friend
Didn't want to be your lover
Didn't need someone to lean on
Didn't wish for you to tell me
You'd be someone to depend on
But look at me now
Like an addict over you
I try to intervene between
My sanity and fantasy
Still I lose every time
I've begun to lose count of the
Times a day you cross my mind
I didn't ask for this aching pain
Didn't want to break away
I grew comfortable in the norm
But it hurts too much to stay
Look at you now
Saying things you never would
At least that's what you told me
Was it all misunderstood?
Was this a part of your plan?
Was I the prey in your predatory scam?
I didn't ask to get on this rollercoaster
Strapped in now with no escape
For every high point
The plunging let downs
Never let me feel safe
Look at us now
Unrecognizable to each other
Perhaps some distance may
Help regain our composure
Because right now I detest you
Right now I resent you
I didn't ask for any of this
So I'm giving it all back to you

Cliffhanger

Standing over the edge
Looking down below
My heart is pounding constantly
Pressure enough to make my rib cage blow
It's been a long time coming
Though I've tried to suppress
This uncertainty and confusion
Beating in my chest
I am love and patience
I am fear and pain
I am joy, greatness and freedom
I am the essence of change
I have climbed this mountain
With no safety net or harness
And now it's time for me to jump
Take a gamble into darkness
I pulled the cord and fell for you
So many times before
Maybe that was the problem
I should have said much more
But I have to take this dive for me
Into the abyss
Who knows where I'll end up?
Either way, something will be missed
Maybe we will meet again
Swimming freely together in the
Gorgeous ocean beneath us
Somehow along the way
We lost the electricity between us
And wedges became walls
I am scared to let down
It's like moving backwards in time
I wish I could turn around
I wish I could start our painting over
On a blank canvas
But I have to do this for me

Looking In

I am looking at myself

So foolish over you

But no matter how I try

My actions can't seem to be subdued

I try to reel myself back into reality

But I am stuck in this fantasy

One that will prove to be no good

And just cause a catastrophe

Yet and still I need one more glimpse

One more touch

I feel like I'm addicted, and withdrawn

In need of interventions and such

I can't even save myself

Because deep down I don't want to be saved

I just hope I see the light

Before it gets to be too late

Reality is Perception

What is reality?

I really don't know

Because to me reality is

How far you allow your mind to go

To a crazy person

Where normalcy is never learned

The reality in their head is all they have to earn

Reality should be called perception

Because that's truly what it is

Stealing food to survive

Never crosses the minds of the wealthy

When people are executed

They say to let them burn

But do you think the same ones

Would feel differently if it was their turn?

What ever you go through is your reality

It just all depends on your mentality

You don't know what you don't know

Because reality only goes as far

As your mind allows it to go

The eye is the lamp of the body. If your eyes are
good, you whole body will be full of light.

Matthew 6:22

Memory Card

Filled beyond capacity

No storage room available

I try to retain these mental images, but

My memory card is unable

Deleting valuable data and saving spiritual junk

So busy capturing seemingly important moments

Until my files become undone

Thoughts shaking and rattling reaching critical overload

Sometimes I just need a moment to myself

To comprehend the story being told

But I am not bitter, ungrateful or discounting my many blessings

It's the lessons of one who has been given much

And is required much the same

So if you see me laying down my responsibilities for a moment

I am neither lazy nor weak

I just need to be connected with the charger

To take some time to get back to me

Smoking Ashes

Look at me, go ahead
I know you seethe
With envy and greed
But look at me
I am the hottest flicker
Of the flame
The MVP's here to reign
On your parade
Are you insane to even dream
You can reach this pinnacle?
I may sound cynical but really
Let's be serious
You do not possess the intellect
Or command respect
Gazes intersect and collide
Just to land on me
I write your checks and cash
You in for change
I am the reason for the
Disdain that remains plastered on your face
I am blazing hot
Until I can't stand it
Climbing out of my own skin
To stand next to myself
Only to realize
I never inspired any sparks
I was just smoking ashes....

Behind A Smile (Part 2)

Lies a hidden agenda
Lies a cry in the dark
Lies a woman scorned
Unintentional heartbreak
It's unconventional, but I say
Behind a smile lies
What you think you know
But you really don't know because
The person that gives it to you only allows you to
See as much as the smile wants you to know
Is a lie untold
Is destruction masked by multiple interpretations
Is piece, by piece, by piece of a soul
So lost you start to think you
Were found but no one else sees you
Like "Where's Waldo?"
Is ongoing struggle that has got me tossing
And turning and yearning for
A solution to a problem no more than skin deep
So that's why I pray to the Lord
My soul to keep
Unleashed potential
It's unconventional, but I say
Behind a smile lurks a dark corner
And gloomy valleys of misperception
Of a lesson we all seem to miss
We are imperfect beings striving for perfection
Not polished, not shiny
But gritty and rough
Your soft heart has been callused
And that smile, that beautiful smile
Is just enough, just enough
To make someone in a worse situation feel
Special
While on the inside you crumble

You smile because your mother
Says it's a nice ending to a please or thank you
You smile and say "Yes, Sir"
When you have to work overtime
But smiles are prismatic, multi-facetted
Like a diamond
Look into my eyes for the real remedy
There you will find the truth
And only there you will find you

Hazy Mist

The mist in the air brings back memories

And creates new ones

Reminding me of the things I don't have

The sweet sting is familiar but I still come undone

My senses are discombobulated to the point

Where I smell your touch

Taste your gaze

Visualize the tone of your voice

And hear the expressions on your face

Another spray is released

Into the atmosphere

Damn….realities collide again

And it's not possible to have you here

So I will settle for the next best thing…

If I could capture the good feeling of that mist

And bottle it…I would

Hold it tight and never let go

But as the final molecule falls to the ground

I reluctantly pack my bags and back to reality I go

Vacation

My heart is in an exotic, stunningly radiant place

My mind is in another location

Screaming, pleading with me

Telling me this beautiful place

Could be disastrous for me

I don't want to leave this secluded island

With all of its fancy amenities

But I must…because the reality is…there is no us

Overnight trip to a several night stay

So and so forth until my head begins to ache

I am full of the wine and delicacies provided

But the truth remains…

Although I have enjoyed my stay

This is a place I do not reside

It is a house and not a home

Built with bricks of bliss and pain

What a shame to keep having to reel myself in again.

Reality knocked on the door

But I refused to let it in

Maybe If

Maybe if you didn't look so good
I could learn to let you go
Maybe if I didn't miss your touch
My heart wouldn't grow cold
Maybe if I could be numb to
The pain in your pretty brown eyes
I could turn my back on you
But I can't
I just can't…..Let you go
When to stay or let it go?
Maybe if you didn't wind it up so tight
I could walk out the door
But somehow you always keep me waiting,
And wanting more
I am caught in an angle of moments
Filled with love and pain
And no matter how bad it gets
Or how hard it rains
I still stick around because
You………….woo me
You captivate me
Stimulate me
Sometimes irritate me
And aggravate me
Maybe we'll just let it flow
When to stay or let it go?
I don't want a fair-weather love
Maybe so love
Possibilities of love bring us
Right back to the original question…
When to stay or let it go?

Gray Matter

Who's to say there's a heaven or hell?

Who's going to reward you for what you do now?

And judge if you're doing it well?

Is this why they say that

God is Good and the Devil is Evil?

The way a bullet burns through the skin

Are you really paying for hell now?

And all your life in sin?

Good luck is really God's love

Someone watching you, watching me

From up above

Whatever happens I do my best

Try to live right, just like the rest

Cause no one really knows about the other side

And no one that has died can come back

And tell us which road to take along the ride

Guess Who, Guess What

Can you guess who I am?

Let me give you a hint

Some say I burn your soul so scorched

It'll make your eyes squint

I'm the uninvited guest

But still I come over to visit

Then I decide to stay awhile

Make you question your living

I come in many forms

Drugs, sex, gossip and gambling

If you were smart you wouldn't read the rest

Cause it might send your mind rambling

Scrambling, you can't hide

No, you can't run away

I thought you'd know by now

I'm addiction, destroying lives every day

Dirty Laundry

Do you smell that?
The stench of us reeking?
Like old gym socks and Fritos
Like spoiled milk and rancid meat
So bad you can smell
Us coming before you see us
Or better yet before we even speak
True, we have been cheated,
Ridiculed, mistreated and misused
But you'd think after
Centuries of brutal history
We'd finally get a clue
The funk we exhibit daily
Is not the event of our demise
Because other cultures do it too
But we serve it on a platter
Right before your very eyes
Airing out our dirty laundry
For nations to behold
Not trying to sound preachy
Because this is a we dilemma
And not a you catastrophe
So sit back and let the truth be told
Calling each other niggers
Beyond the comfort of our homes
While we are angered by honkies, chinks and wetbacks
Who guard and cherish their cultures
And who, compared to us
Are not seen nearly as much
On the 10:00 news
In gangster movies

Or heard in violent raps
Scapegoats by definition
But oppressed by willing submission
Some things are better left unsaid
Because it's better to be thought a fool
Than speak and remove all doubt
Character is what we lack
And unlike American Express
It's the one thing we always
Seem to leave home without

Fools (Me or You)

Wisdom once told me
To never argue with fools
Because people from a distance
Can't tell who is who
So I use my better judgment
Although I am only made of flesh
The task seems achievable enough
Until you are put to the test
The woman staying in an abusive relationship
Never knowing her self worth and the
Cowardly man who is the pusher for her addictive hurt...
Which one are you? Which one is me?
What deciphers, from a distance, who the fool should be?
Gruesome violence in a vengeful
Moment of malice
Was it really worth it to have
Your soul calloused?
Which one are you? Which one am I?
What will the verdict be after I testify?
Getting caught up in devilish snares
Following the wrong paths
Listening to the wrong voice
And peace of mind is rare
Again, I wonder.....which one is me? Which one is you?
Who will be the one to play the fool?
Maybe it is both, maybe one removed
Maybe one reformed or the outsider too.
What will people say when they turn to look at you?
Will it be so easy to recognize a wise man from a fool?

What a beautiful sight/But only in the environment of freedom/All of the lights shining brightly for all to see/Am I the only one who sees this entropy?

Carlos Harleaux

Blurred Vision

Looking into the rays of sun
All I see is empty promises
And the portent of rain to come
The beginnings of coming undone
Feel a sprinkle here and there
The clouds are hugged up like we used to be
But producing a disaster I never thought we could
This storm has stripped us bare
Windshield wipers working double time
Trying to provide clarity to the inevitable
Prove everybody wrong by standing in this puddle
These muddy waters have somehow made us blind
Hail is piercing against my skin
A warning I should have heeded
I'm slowly running out of fuel
Drenched in heartache once again
Now I am traveling on foot
Determined to reach my destination
Where the hell am I going anyway?
Tell me since you claim to know me like a book
Detours we thought would give us comfort
Have gotten us off track
And now our sight is so aloof
We may never find our way back

All That Glitters

All that glitters ain't gold
Still I tried to find the brilliance in you
I flipped and turned and scraped and burned
Off the ugly so that all I could see was greatness
No matter how many flaws there were
Between the 1st, 2nd, 3rd, 4th and 5th surfaces
I gritted my teeth to grin and bear it
And drape and wear it upon my shoulders
Like a regal cloak and it's just a joke
That everybody's laughing at but me
I endured the growing pains because the
Light shined so brightly on you
Blinded by my own line of sight
And all I could wrap my
Thoughts around was you
Reaching in the night when
I know you're not there
Feeling my leg vibrating
Thinking it's you calling
But there's no phone in my pocket
So I've got the other hand reaching
Towards this socket to plug my charger in
Just in case you decide to say hello
This is a pathetic place to be in

Yet I turn the key and let myself into
This mess everyday
Here, memories entrap my train of thought
Until the clutter makes me feel like I'm on
An episode of Hoarders: Insane Edition
Packing up this trash that I just can't
Seem to part with
So it just sits as I reminisce on a possession
I was too possessive of to have never even owned
All that glitters ain't gold
Though I made you out to be something like
Platinum coated morning dew
Until I turned the lights down
To a shade of truth
And realized you're just fool's gold
Under a dim point of view

Erase

Ever wish you could erase moments in time?

Just a few back spaces, a simple draw of the line?

Words spoken can not be retracted

And actions committed can not be reinterpreted

The tongue is the most powerful muscle that

Always seems to get us in the most trouble

It speaks the heart and reveals what the mind is processing

Without filter

It cuts deeper than the most intentional physical blow

Burns further than the third degree

If only life was so simple to white out the mess we made

From day to day

Game Over

Every morning I awake
To yet another round
A higher level, given by
A higher power
While the image of
Death lays abound
I don't have to insert two quarters
To reload my guns
Blow on the console
Or reboot the system
He gives me brand new mercies
And single handedly
Annihilates my enemies
With His fail proof navigation system
Sometimes this game gets
A little taxing
We all have different destinations
But knowing He never relaxes
Keeps me going
And I reach for the mushrooms
To make me grow stronger in Him
And sometimes I wonder
What would happen if
He froze the screen?
Eliminated the daily bonus rounds
And second chances?
What if He never let us see the victory
For cancelling the mystery?
These questions I can't answer
Alone, but I keep my owner's manual handy
And I'm just grateful to still
Be in the game

Buzz

Bzzzz….I hear you coming
Before you even turn the corner
I cringe at the thought
Like nails on a chalk board…of you
You who thinks of no one else
But selfishly crafting ulterior motives
You, who have no authority over me
But somehow in your simple mind
You think you own me and my reactions
But I won't be the pebble in your sandbox games
You are the dirt from my feet washed down the drain
I gain nothing from the possibility of thinking
One day you'll change
So I remove myself from the situation
Where only one fool remains
Splat…..I thought I got rid of you
Yet you resurface again like oil and water
But you fail to remember I will always end up on top
Get over yourself; you are not the cream of the crop
The demise of your backbiting is upon you…..lookout!
The smack down is upon you
But I'm not bitter, nor will I lose any sleep
This is just a notification, an invitation to you
To say how you really feel
What you really think, but I know you won't
So shoo fly

Another Love

I could move forward with my life
But it's just not the same
Sometimes, I think of
How perfect it would be
To have it all back again
And sometimes I just lay awake
Thinking of you
Cause baby I could have anybody
But that's not me and you
Another girl for me just won't do
Another girl ain't the same as me and you
Baby, can't you see
There's no other love for me
Another love ain't enough
Cause I could have anybody
But that's not you and me
I could push you to the side
Try to block you out my mind
But how many times I've failed
I keep coming back to you
With you is where I wanna be
Somebody else won't replace you and me
Cause baby I could have anybody
But that's not me and you
Another girl for me just won't do
Another girl ain't the same as me and you
Baby, can't you see
There's no other love for me
Another love ain't enough
Cause I could have anybody
But that's not you and me

Because Of You

It's all because of you that

I'm so skeptical to trust

Don't want to give my all again

After me and you stopped being us

It's because of you

I can't see a good thing coming

Blind to brighter days

Settling for what is much less than nothing

Because of you

I am full of self doubt

Drowning out this noise

Since the silence is too loud

All the while I failed to face

The harshly frigid reality

While I was pointing a finger at you

There were three pointing back at me

"Blindfolded bliss/With no compass to guide/Is meaningless worth/Like a dressed-up lie."

Carlos Harleaux

Don't Know

How can you learn to love
When all you see is hate?
If this is all you see
It's all you know
And love, for you, you really don't know
How do you believe in yourself
When others constantly put you down?
If this is all you get
It's all you know
And confidence, for you, you really don't know
How do you learn to have peace
If all around you is violent?
If this is all you endure
It's all you know
And peace, for you, you really don't know
Personalities are shaped by experiences
And if all you experience are bad times
How do you ever know how to turn
Something bad into something good?
Sometimes people can't change their situations
Because all they know tells them
They never could

The Gates of Destiny

The gate swings
But with no hinges
Because it is interchangeable
The breeze of destiny that
Opens and closes the gate
Depends on the spirits of the
Unattainable
And how do you know
Which path to take
When everybody's buzzing in your ear
Reminding you, reminding you
Memories, do you remember when,
Of your mistakes?
So, the question you may ask
Is how do you walk through
A gate that never truly opens or closes?
How can you walk on faith
When the water's not frozen?
I wanna be, I wanna be like
Me?
No one wants to follow self
But will willingly walk into the
Deathtrap set for somebody else
The gate is interchangeable
The breeze of destiny that
Opens and closes the gate
Depends on
The spirits of the unattainable
The gates that lock up innocent people
Searching behind bars
The gates that we build daily
To suppress our soul's scars
But if we fail to see
Before the end of the night
That the focus is not the gate
But solely the light
How can we really reach destiny?

Missionary Love

My mission that I choose to accept is one I complete

But always regret

If I could escape it, I would

Without turning back

But no matter how bad it gets

I keep running back

Living in this fantasy

Hoping one day you'll change

Wasted all this time

And things still stay the same

Blinded by my desire to change you

Somehow I started believing I was

Supposed to save you

But your bags are weighing me down

And at the end of the day

You're not even around

My mission that I choose to accept

Is one I complete, but always regret

My mission that I choose to accept

Is one I should have never kept

Stronghold

Sometimes I feel like my chest is going under

The lightning and the thunder

Is warning of the rumble, I stumble

And crumble, digging my way out of this quicksand

In a strange land, unfamiliar territory

I can't sustain on my own

My soul is getting hungry

This ship is setting sail

I gotta jump deck

With all these intersections

My mental state's a wreck

I pray I come to my senses before it's too late

The clock is ticking, and I can't help but wish

That the sun would start to shine

And erase this from my mind

No one to really turn to

We all got our own issues

Especially when the ones to confide in

Going through it with you

Nowhere to look but up

It seems I lost my focus

I'm in a war to get it back

And redefine my purpose

The Weakest Link

My brother, my brother
Look what you do
We down in the gutter
So we look up to you
Just pushin, just pushin
That death on the streets
My brother, oh brother
You are the weakest link
My sister, my sister
Look at your face
Flying without wings
Inner beauty erased
Don't tell me, don't tell me
That's all you can be
My sister, oh sister
You are the weakest link
My teacher, my teacher
Look what you feed
You give no motivation
Why should we feel the need?
Just going, just going
Through the motions
Can't you see?
My teacher, oh teacher
You are the weakest link
Who's pointing, Who's pointing?
I look at myself
Sometimes the space is you
Not somebody else
Reflections, reflections
Now what do I see
Who's pointing, who's pointing?
The weakest link is me
His children, His children
We never seem to listen
For we know not the extent

Of the blessings we're missing
Now His children, His children
What would you say?
What would you think?
If He told you, He told you
Depart from me, my child
You are the weakest link, GOODBYE!

Until The Next Time

Packed all my bags
Put your pictures in a box
Placed your letters to the side
In safe keeping with a lock
This time will be different
This time I will break away
This time buys time until
The next time is the last time
I decide to stay
Me and you are a toxic concoction
Caught up and stretched in this
Tangled web where I am
At your mercy to untangle me
The heart wants what it wants
And I want you to the point that it hurts
I need you close like putting on a new shirt
No wife beater
You have to understand
That this is final, no turning back
So I keep moving forward
With agony lighting my jagged path
Until my internal compass
Trips me up and I head back sour
Head back south where familiar heartbreak
Is more comfortable than
The unfamiliarity of new beginnings
So I try to explore these new beginnings with you
Because failed attempts are better than
New ones without you
So it seems my mind is bursting
At the seams
Trying to hold together broken pieces of yesterday
But this time will be different
This time I will break away
No need to buy time
Until the last next time
My exit is here, the toll's already been paid

Tired

It's time to tell the truth
It's time to keep it real and
Let you know exactly how I feel
Time out for being politically correct
And holding back
So, oh well, here goes...
I'm tired of going unnoticed
Not for lights and recognition
But mutual dedication is what always
Seems to be missing
I'm tired of you hiding behind these walls
I've been here all along,
So show your face and speak your peace
If you really got balls
Tired of analyzing so much
Even when I'm right
Sometimes it is a luxury to
Live a crazy person's life
Tired of making something out of nothing and
Nothing outta something
Unbeknownst to me, it just wears me down
You think you know
But you have no idea
What stands before you is just the tip of
The iceberg
I'm tired of wasting time and space
So let's avoid repetition
And move expeditiously

I'm tired and when you look
You can probably see it in my eyes
Battle scars in a war of my own state of mind
I'm running low on fuel and peace is $30 a gallon
But this time it's different
Cause it's ok if I have to push my car in the light
Just so I can sleep at night
But for now I'll take a nap
While I'm at the red light

Clocking Out

I've been working over time
And I'm starting to notice the tension
From doing things that aren't even
Specified in my job description
I've dipped too many times in my 401K
Now I'm left with nothing to show
For being your personal slave

This job of pleasing you
Has finally run its course
No 2 weeks notice
I resign with no remorse
Gotta leave, gotta go
My heart is aching, sore
I decline any promotions
Just can't take this no more

Doing all the grunge work
While you just sit on your ass
Under these conditions
Love surely won't last
My watch just stopped working
I think I need to take a break and
Today I'm leaving early
No matter what the supervisor says

This job of pleasing you
Has finally run its course
No 2 weeks notice
I resign with no remorse
Gotta leave, gotta go
My heart is aching, sore
I decline any promotions
Just can't take this no more

Some people say that quitters never win
But in my case, I'd rather
Be unemployed
Then caught up in this tailspin
They say you never know
What you got 'til it's gone
But I know you gotta feel it
Every time that you're alone
Just be sure to shred the incriminating evidence
Before the next employee
Comes along…I'm clocking out

The Taste of Love

Like summer sweet Butter Pecan ice cream

On hot Dutch apple crumb pie

Love used to taste like this

You remember when love felt like this?

I savor the flavor of

Intricate memories

I breathe them in my sleep

And embrace their awakening

And still I stand

Confessions of love's past

Who has lived to taste a thought so fond?

It is I who stands alone and stunned

Wondering will I ever see that captivating sensation…

Will I ever hear the sweet and sour senses

Of pleasure?

Who will by my supernova amidst

Turbulent seas?

Will I ever touch the sight of effervescent joy…

Again?

Remembering Love

Sound of Silence

There is not a sound to be heard here

But the beating of my heart

In this stillness is where

It all seems to start

Holding on to what I believe

And defining my own destiny

But silence creeps in and its

Motives have other plans for me

So I occupy my time with noisy endeavors

And band aids to make me think I'm feeling better

Then I peel away the layers

But only when no one else can see

To take time to understand the one who is the inner me

There's no coasting through this journey

The ride isn't always smooth

But every day I don't give up

It gives me that much more to prove

For I will now confront this silence head on

And deal with what has been suppressed

You have no rights here, silence

You are under arrest

"My heart bleeds/Ink to paper/But I share it
now/Instead of later"

Carlos Harleaux

The Sleep-In Generation

We were born without
Wait a minute, scratch that
I ain't had my nap yet
We were born with a silver spoon
Curved so deep you could
Sit the moon in it
Don't touch me
Stop all that noise
I'm still learning how to walk
With balance and poise
I'll call you when I wake up
Whenever that will be
But don't count on it though
Cause I didn't go to bed 'til 3:00
Yeah I know I gotta go to work
But I'm their best employee
Just last week I increased profits by…
Oh no, not again
Wait let me see
Oh, just forget it
Just call me later
Cause I didn't go to sleep 'til 3:00
When I wake up
I'll catch up with the world
Running past me

Angels Unaware

When you curse me
You don't know
What you've done
You've disrespected an angel
Just because I'm silent
Doesn't mean that you are victorious
Because I have a ruler
Who, above all is glorious
When you tease me
You don't know
Who you've messed with
You've mistreated an angel
An angel, unaware
Just because I smile
Doesn't mean I like you
But I am commanded to love you
This is not checkers
And you are not the king of me
So go ahead and do what you do
Because His promise
Will forever be true
But, when you plot against me
What a mistake you've made
Because when you mess with me
You mess with my Father
And that will surely
Get yourself played!

Broken

Shattered to pieces
This is my thesis
That I have perfected over and over
Every time I step outside
My soul gets colder and colder
Until I'm frozen, and broken
Unspoken like a gigantic iceberg
After awhile I get numb to the pain
Though I still feel the reign
And through it all I maintain
Sustain and contain
Just to rearrange these broken pieces
So they are less visible to the opponent
Whoever that may be
Only to look inside of my steamy window
To see that probably all along it was me
I didn't know, I seem to grow
All the while my seeds are sown
All the while my seeds are sown
Chipped and weathered
And frayed and tattered
Outsides are polished
Insides feel battered
Self inflicted, so addicted
To the things that don't love me
Devastating, captivating
Simply shattered to pieces
This is my unedited thesis

Through My Eyes

Through my eyes
Sparks fly
Bright with intensity
Dark with mystery
In my sight
I see greatness
Destined for great places
Through my stare
I dare those who come
Close to find out
The secret message
Through my vision
With precision, repetition
Is not usual
Through my gaze
I see through the storm
To make it past
The rainy days
And through the passion
Of my soul, I feel free